Whispers of the Soul

Whispers of the Soul

Christian Poetry

Book Five of the Heart and Soul Christian Poetry Collection

Esselle Davis

Whispers of the Soul
Christian Poetry
Book Five of the Heart and Soul Christian Poetry Collection
First Edition
ISBN: 9798685772947
© 2020 Esselle Davis
All rights reserved

DEDICATION

Whispers of the Soul
Christian Poetry
is dedicated to:

My husband Tony
My daughter Mandy
The memory of my Mama, Mary
The memory of my Daddy, Doyle

PREFACE

My journey to writing poetry began when I wanted to send an online greeting to a friend of mine. I couldn't find anything that I liked, or anything that had the message I wanted to send to her. I had a thought to write my own and I thought about what I wanted to say. I wanted it to be something about an angel, so I looked at many images of angels and I finally found one. Looking at that particular picture gave me the thoughts that eventually became a poem. I had managed to write one poem and tried my hand at writing a few more. After receiving encouragement from family and friends I continued to write. There have been times I moved away from writing, but I always come back to it. I find peace in writing and enjoy my time spent writing.

14 And as Moses lifted up the serpent in the wilderness, even so must the Son of man be lifted up:
15 That whosoever believeth in him should not perish, but have eternal life.
16 For God so loved the world, that he gave his only begotten Son, that whosoever believeth in him should not perish, but have everlasting life.
17 For God sent not his Son into the world to condemn the world; but that the world through him might be saved.

John 3:16 King James Version

Contents

FLAME OF HOPE

A flame of hope
Burns within
It was lit the day Jesus
Saved me from sin

I prayed to Him
He heard my plea
He saved my soul
And set me free

He lit a flame
Down in my soul
He entered my heart
And made me whole

Sometimes I may falter
Sometimes I may fall
But the Savior's love
I do recall

Then I pray to Jesus
Whom I adore
Then my flame
He does restore

So you see my flame may flicker

When I'm filled with doubt

But thanks to Jesus

It has never gone out

LORD GUIDE ME

Lord guide me
As I go to and fro
Let me share Your love Lord
With everyone I know

Don't let me be tempted
By Satan's distractions
Lord guide me
In all of my actions

Don't let my words
Be harsh or bleak
Lord guide me
As I speak

Don't let my thoughts
Be sour or evil
Lord guide me
And protect me from upheaval

When my day is over
And I face the night
Lord guide me
With Your beautiful light

As I ready myself for bed

I pray and know You hear my plea

When tomorrow arrives

Lord guide me

ANGEL OF HOPE

I'm an angel of hope
Sent from Heaven above
God told me to protect you
With all of His love

He wants me to keep
You so close to Him
He forbids me to leave
You out on a limb

God does not want you
Drowning in sin
His Son is the lifeboat
And will welcome you in

I am here to remind you
In times of strife
From the blood of Jesus
You gained eternal life

Whenever troubles beset you
And you're feeling down
Cast your eyes upon Jesus
And think of the crown

That upon your head

One day you'll be wearing

Because Jesus the Savior

Is so loving and caring

WALK WITH ME TODAY

Lord as I face the morning
And get ready to journey on my way
I will take the time to ask you
Walk with me today

I may face hardships
I may stumble and fall
But I know You are there for me
If on You I do call

I may be filled with happiness
And my heart be filled with joy
But I want You there with me
As the good times I enjoy

I may be met with sorrow
My spirit to You may cry
But Lord I'll take comfort
In knowing You are nearby

Lord each day will be different
Though some things may be the same
But I know I will make it through
By trusting in Your name

So Lord as I prepare
To go along my way
I come to You asking
Walk with me today

THE LORD IS MY SHEPHERD

The Lord is my Shepherd
He guides me each day
He is there to lead me
As I go along my way

He is there with me
My steps to guide
Peace to my heart
He does provide

But if I falter
He will hear my plea
He will pick me up
And carry me

Through whatever hardship
I may face
By believing in Him
I am saved by grace

By His blood
My soul was bought
He gives me comfort
When I'm distraught

I am a part of
His precious flock
He is my shepherd
He is my rock

THE DAY YOU DIED

Hearts were broken
Tears were cried
Sorrow filled many
The day you died

For those, who had
To let you go
Your passing left them
Filled with woe

In their sorrow
Comfort they receive
Because they know
In Jesus, you did believe

Even though your death
Fills them with pain
They know you are now walking
Along Heavens golden lane

Their love for you
Will never cease
But they know
You are now at peace

Because as death came to you

Angels were by your side

Jesus was waiting

The day you died

THE MASTER'S LOVING HAND

In the grand scheme of things
I may be just a grain of sand
But I've been touched
By the Master's loving hand

Jesus is the Master
That I speak of
He gave me a gift
He gave me His love

When I opened my heart
And let him in
He saved my soul
And forgave my sin

I am not perfect
And here on earth I will never be
But I have a friend
Who walks daily with me

When I make mistakes
And stumble and fall
I pray to Jesus
And on him I call

When it seems that on my own

I can not stand

I call out to Jesus and am lifted

By the Master's loving hand

BAPTISM OF JESUS

John preached of repentance
In the wilderness
Many people came to him
Their sins to confess

John told the people there was
One coming mightier than he
John knew that Jesus was the one
Who could set the soul free

John knew his position
And of this he didn't boast
He told the people Jesus would
Baptize them with the Holy Ghost

One day at the river Jordan
John saw this man
Jesus came to be baptized
To fulfill God's master plan

When the baptism of Jesus
Had taken place
As Jesus came up
And water dripped from His face

As Jesus looked up

Into the sky

There was coming from God

A wonderful reply

For God had been watching

From His throne above

He sent from Heaven the Spirit

In the form of a dove

The people who were there

Knew Jesus was the one

For God's voice rang out

"This is my beloved Son"

I HAVE A MARY HEART I LIVE IN A MARTHA WORLD

I have a Mary heart
I live in a Martha world
Sometimes things push and pull me
It seems I'm being whirled

I want to be like Mary
And sit at the master's feet
But I'm more like Martha
With so many tasks I have to meet

I want to be like Mary
And spend time with God's precious Son
But I'm more like Martha
There are many things to be done

I want to be like Mary
And hear what the Master has to say
But I'm more like Martha
There are not enough hours in the day

I may be more like Martha
By my duties my time is blurred
But I make the time to be like Mary
And spend time with God's Holy word

Here on earth I may be like Martha
Trying to meet the daily demands
While desiring to be like Mary
And feel the touch of the Master's hands

One day I will go to Heaven
When God the Father says it is time
I will then live in a place
With beauty so sublime

Then I will no longer be like Martha
With many duties I have to meet
Praise God I will be like Mary
And bow at my Savior's feet

WAITING FOR HIS RETURN

When I was saved
Jesus came into my heart
He gave me life and
A brand new start

I now have the promise
Of eternal life
I have a friend to go to
When I feel strife

Jesus is coming back
Just like He said
A Heavenly feast
Will soon be spread

He will take the saved
To their brand new home
To go there
Nevermore to roam

No one knows the
Hour or day
When Jesus will return
To take God's children away

The day is coming
It could be soon
Morning or night
Or afternoon

I am ready and waiting
For Jesus to come get me
Oh what a glorious time
That time will be

When Jesus calls
I'll go to Heaven so fair
I'll see beauty
Beyond compare

This day is one
For which I yearn
But for now I'm patiently
Waiting for His return

ROAD TO GLORY

There is a journey
With a wonderful story
I am now walking
The road to glory

I began this journey
While on my knees
Jesus entered my heart
And put me at ease

Sometimes the Devil
Has led me astray
The Holy Spirit has helped me
To go back the right way

Sometimes the path
May seem dark and long
But Jesus gives me light
And keeps me strong

Sometimes I may be sad
And even be filled with strife
But Jesus will be with me
All of my life

He gives me happiness
That the lost can not feel
For I was bought with His blood
Which is precious and real

Jesus is with me
As onward I go
He gave His life
So that God's love I could know

When my life on earth
Comes to an end
I will go to Heaven
And see Jesus my truest friend

My journey will be over
And my work on earth done
Then I will live forever with God
And Jesus His precious Son

GOD CALLED YOU HOME

God looked down from Heaven
He saw you filled with pain
He decided your suffering was over
With us you would no longer remain

So God called your precious name
And your body gave way to death
Jesus was there waiting
As you took your last breath

When your last breath left you
With Jesus you went
You are now at peace
Living happy and content

You are living in Heaven
Your wonderful new home
The pain that you had here
Is now no longer known

You can now see loved ones
Gone on before
As they walk along
Heavens bright shore

Of course I will miss you
But my heart is at peace
For God gives me comfort
That will never cease

I will think of you often
As I go along life's way
But I will see you again
Some glorious day

For I too have been saved
By God's amazing grace
Jesus has wrapped me
In His loving embrace

When my time comes
I am ready to die
I will meet you in Heaven
And we will never say goodbye

YOUR HEAVENLY FLIGHT

You fought death
At every turn
While for Heaven
Your spirit did yearn

You thought God
Was moving slow
Asking us to
Let you go

Your legs were contracted
You could not walk
At the end
You could no longer talk

You were far sicker
Than anyone knew
But you had faith God
Would carry you through

Loved ones in Heaven
Their faces you did see
Holding your hand up
Saying to God come get me

But family here
You were not ready to forget
You would then shake your head
And say no not yet

You gave a good fight
But when your time came
God sent the death angel
Your life to claim

At the moment of death
Your eyes filled with delight
Your spirit was set free
For its Heavenly flight

You are now in Heaven
Your treasures you can view
I hope you knew
How much we loved you

JESUS

Jesus is my Savior
My redeemer and friend
He loves me with a love
That knows no end

He is the anchor
That keeps me steady
When I need Him
He is always ready

To extend to me
A helping hand
He is the rock
On which I stand

He gives me a peace
That to some is unknown
He has provided me a way
To the Heavenly throne

Jesus always has time
To listen to my prayer
He sends me comfort
I know He's always there

If I am scared
Jesus can calm my fears
When I am sad
He can dry my tears

When I am weary and tired
And feel that I can't go on
I can call on Jesus
Because now I'm never alone

He is always with me
And walks by my side
If I lose my way
He's there my steps to guide

He will come
To get me one day
Then with Him forever
In Heaven I'll stay

MARRIAGE SUPPER OF THE LAMB

I have reservations for an event
That one day will arrive
It is because of this event
My heart and soul do thrive

I was invited to this event
When my heart the Spirit did seize
I accepted the invitation
And met Jesus on my knees

I asked Him to save me
And give peace to my soul
He forgave all my sins
And He then made me whole

Jesus paid the price
On the cross of Calvary
This invitation is available to all
And the cost of it is free

To receive your invitation
To this glorious event
Get down on your knees
And humbly repent

Open your self up
And let Jesus in your heart
And from this wicked world
You will be set apart

Then I will see you
In Heaven someday
There with God the Father
Forever we will stay

We will look upon
God's wonderful face
For we were saved
By His marvelous grace

We will be in the presence
Of the great I Am
There to dine in Heaven
At the marriage supper of the Lamb

MY BLESSINGS

Lord thank you for the blessings
That you send my way
I should be thanking you
All through the day

Lord I want to thank you
For saving my soul
You gave me hope
And made me whole

Lord, You are God's
One and only Son
The blessing of my salvation
Is the most special one

Lord thank you
For my dear family
I love them so much
They are precious to me

Lord thank you
For the roof over my head
When I need rest
I thank you for my bed

Lord thank you
For the food I eat
Thank you for the shoes
I wear on my feet

Lord thank you for
The clothes I wear
Thank you for
Your loving care

Lord all of your blessings
I could never recall
There are so many
I couldn't name them all

Lord in each of my blessings
I find delight
May the joy of them
Never leave my sight

THANK YOU FOR LOVING ME

Dear Jesus there is so much
That I could thank you for
I am happier now with You in my life
Than I was before

I was tangled in
The webs of sin
I had no hope
Or peace within

But I came to you
On bended knee
I asked for Your forgiveness
And Lord You gave salvation to me

You are there with me
Through all that I face
There is nothing anywhere
That could ever take Your place

You give me comfort
In times of sorrow
You give me hope
For a bright new tomorrow

You are with me
When I am in pain
You wrap me in Your care
And with me You remain

You are also with me
When I am filled with joy
You bless me with happiness
And Your peace I enjoy

You blessed me with a family
That loves me so true
Jesus I am also thankful
They know Your love too

Jesus I could never thank you
For all that You have given me
For when I call on You
Lord You hear my plea

Sweet Jesus I offer myself
Your servant to be
To say to you
Thank you for loving me

SALVATION

We live in a world
Filled with wickedness and sin
But Jesus God's Son
Can be our dearest friend

Jesus came to earth
Many years ago
So that the glory of God
We all could know

Jesus hanged on a cross
And faced ridicule and shame
He will forgive you of sin
If your believe on His name

Ask God to forgive you
And let Jesus in your heart
Then from God the Father
You will never depart

He will send the Spirit
To guide you each day
Because the devil
Will try to lead you astray

Satan wants you to think
God's word is a lie
The will of the Father
He wants you to deny

Between God and man
Sin has caused a great rift
Salvation through Jesus
Is God's greatest gift

With His wonderful salvation
In Heaven you will dwell
Without Jesus you will face
An eternity in Hell

When your life is over
And your take your last breath
You will lay down this body
With your eyes closed in death

If you die without Jesus
Forever in Hell you'll burn
If you are covered by His blood
An eternity in Heaven you'll earn

HEAVEN

When Jesus ascended
He went to prepare
Our new home
In Heaven so fair

Before He left He promised
That He would for us return
It is for His coming
Our hearts and souls do yearn

Jesus will come for us
One day in a cloud
The trumpet will sound
Ever so loud

When we meet Jesus
Up in the sky
To our new home
Away we will fly

When we enter in
At the pearly white gate
We will know that Jesus made possible
This wonderful fate

We will walk upon on streets
Paved with pure gold
The wonders of Heaven
Are ours to behold

A mansion will be
Our brand new home
Heartache and sadness
No more will be known

We will walk beside
The river of life
Up in Heaven
There will be no more strife

We will meet our loved ones
Gone on before
In Heaven
We will live forevermore

In Heaven there will be
No sorrow or pain
When you accept Jesus
Heaven is what you gain

STORMS OF LIFE

As I sometimes face
The storms of life
I may suffer
Heartbreak and strife

But God the Father
In Heaven above
Will give me peace
Through His pure love

God sent His Son
To die for all man's sin
Jesus is the best friend
There ever has been

Jesus will never leave me
He will always be there
He will keep me wrapped
In His tender loving care

The storms of life may toss me
And turn me about
But the power of Jesus
I will never doubt

Jesus is my shelter
In the time of the storm
When I accepted Him as Savior
My life He did transform

So now when trouble comes
And the waves of sorrow roll high
I call on Jesus
And He hears my cry

He wraps me in His love
So safe and so strong
I was bought by His blood
And to Him I belong

This storm is now over
I am safe and secure
With the help of my Savior
This storm I did endure

Jesus has given me peace
That to some is unknown
He always by my side
I am never alone

CALVARY

Jesus was tried
And sentenced to die
There were those that thought
He was telling a lie

They did not believe
That He was God's Son
They thought if they killed Him
They would be done

So to carry out
His Father's will
Jesus made the trip
Up Calvary's hill

As they nailed Him to the cross
You could hear the terrible sound
Then they raised the cross up
And placed it in the ground

As Jesus hanged there
For everyone to see
He cried "My God My God
Why hast thou forsaken me"

Jesus could have called angels
To free Him from the cross
But He knew if He did
We would all be lost

So Jesus hanged there on the cross
And suffered and died
As blood and water
Spilled from His side

Jesus said "It is finished"
As His head began to nod
The centurion said
"Truly this was the Son of God"

By the blood that day
That fell upon the ground
We can be saved
And our lives turned around

When we accept Jesus
We will see heaven someday
For on that cruel cross
Jesus chose to stay

TO BE ABSENT FROM THE BODY

God has taken
Your partner in life
He did not do it
To fill you with strife

She had reached the point
That her life's work was done
She is now living in the presence
Of God and His Son

God knows your sadness
And your dismay
He knows that during grief
Your mood will be gray

But Jesus will be there
Each day for you
He knows your heartache
And He will carry you through

During the times of grief
That you will face
Jesus will comfort you
In His loving embrace

You can turn to Jesus
And on Him you can lean
He will give you peace
Calming and serene

I know you will miss her each day
Every hour
But Jesus will comfort you with
His infinite power

She will remain with you in the memories
Deep in your heart
You will see her again in Heaven
Then you will never be apart

So until the pain fades
And happy memories take its place
Let the next thought
Bring joy to your face

Your partner is now in Heaven
Living in sweet accord
To be absent from the body
Is to be present with the Lord

I BECAME A CHRISTIAN

I became a Christian
When I let Jesus in my heart
The gift of Salvation
To me He did impart

I was saved
By God's amazing grace
The misery of my soul
Comfort did replace

Jesus washed away my sin
And filled my heart with peace
Day by day my love for Him
Continues to increase

Jesus is now a friend
Who knows my every care
No matter what I need
He is always there

There have been good times
And there have been bad
There are times I am happy
There are times I am sad

Jesus is by my side
In all that I do
If times get too tough
He carries me through

I will still sin
And sometimes I will fall
Jesus will lift me up
If on Him I will call

I am not perfect just saved by grace
Through faith in Jesus, God's Son
He will be with me
Till my life's race is run

When I became a Christian
I was not promised times with no strife
But I was given the promise
Of a joyous eternal life

So now when I die
I will go to Heaven above
I will live in a place
Filled with beauty and love

FOREVER SEPTEMBER

Daddy you entered this life
One September day
As a cute little boy
With your siblings you did play

Many years later
When I finally came along
Adopted, I may have been
But, to you and Mama I did belong

I remember many things
You lovingly taught me
You have been gone nine years
In my mind, your face I still see

Your favorite season was autumn
Not too hot or too cold
The colors of the leaves
You loved to behold

Maybe, autumn was your favorite
Because it was the season of your birth
Maybe, it was because you loved to see
Leaves fall upon the earth

You gave your heart to God, one night
As we put up a Christmas tree
You were ecstatic with your salvation
For you knew one day, Heaven you would see

In pain you had asked
For us all to pray
God would send the death angel
To take you away

You left this life
On a warm July night
As your spirit was set free
For its heavenly flight

Daddy your love and lessons
I will never forget
I imagine your face was aglow
When your Savior you met

The happiness autumn brought you
I will always remember
I hope that in Heaven for you
It's forever September

SINKING IN LIFE'S SEA

The darkness closes in
My path is no longer bright
I sit here and contemplate
My soul's ebbing light

Upon the sea of life
My ship, does still sail
But the waves of unrest, pound me
I fear, soon the hull will fail

The waves of sadness crash
Crash against my side
My ship breaks apart
I am in the rising tide

Sadness grabs and pulls me
Slowly pulls me under
Will I sink and drown this time
I cannot help, to wonder

Above the waters surface
My head carefully bobs
Deep within my soul
Are rising mournful sobs

I try to cry out for help
But I feel so alone
It is the worst feeling
I have ever known

My voice has gone silent
I cannot make a sound
By the troubles of life
I have been bound

Will I win this battle?
It seems I'm on the brink
Will I swim away?
Or will I finally sink?

From deep within my soul
For help I implore
Then I see a light
On the distant shore

The light now moves closer
Someone heard my plea
Soon I will be rescued
From this dark and murky sea

A strong hand pulls me

Pulls me from despair
I know I have help
Jesus heard my prayer

Stormy waves now calm
At the Savior's behest
In His strong arms
I can now find rest

In this life there are troubles
Some will never cease
But in Christ my Savior
I can always find peace

The waves of life are unable
To lead me to my slaughter
My Savior's there to rescue me
My Lifeguard walks on water

THE HEART MAY WHISPER BUT THE SOUL WILL SCREAM

I walked into the little church, on a beautiful, Sunday morn
What on earth was I doing there, my feelings, were mixed and torn
Churches and religion, I had always spurned
But, a friend had invited me, for my soul they were concerned

They had told me about Jesus, and how He loved me so
They had asked where I'd spend, eternity, did I truly know?
They said Jesus was their Savior, they also called Him Lord
But I was a good person, so their words I ignored

I had only been to church, a few times, before
Not knowing what to expect, I took the seat closest to the door
At the time I didn't realize, I was lost, broken, and unsaved
My soul needed relief, by my sins I was, enslaved

Hymns began the service, it was a beautiful serenade
Before the preacher stood, heartfelt prayers were prayed
People gathered in the altar, to pray for the lost
Praying they would understand, sin had a heavy cost

The preacher gave the message, the Spirit told him what to say
He preached that we would all, face eternity some day
He preached in our life, we would walk our chosen path

And at our death we would face, God's love or His wrath

He preached about Jesus, and the sacrifice He gave
He said if we accepted Him, Jesus our soul would save
He preached on Heaven's beauty, and the Savior's unending love
He told how the saved, would live in Heaven above

He warned about Satan, who wants to lead us all astray
And keep us from walking, along, the straight and narrow way
He also told of Hell, and the horror it contains
He wanted to see the lost, break free of Satan's chains

The preacher said the choice we made, would determine, where we'd dwell
In the beauty of Heaven, or, in the misery of Hell
I then felt a gentle tug, like, a whisper, from my heart
Calling me to Jesus, so, I could make a brand new start

The preacher, closed the message, the congregation softly sang
The calling of the Spirit, from deep within me it rang
As the altar call was given, white knuckled, I gripped the pew
The Spirit, was speaking to me, telling me what to do

The Spirit, called insistently, I was filled with unrest
I felt that my heart would beat, from within my chest
The Spirit continued calling, with my lost soul, It did deal

I thought I would soon explode, from what It made me feel

I held on for dear life, I ignored, the Spirit's call
Thinking that I had more time, I continued there to stall
I knew I wasn't Heaven bound, in my lost, and broken state
The choice I made, there that day, forever, sealed my fate

I looked toward, the altar, it seemed to be miles away
The distance appeared too far, to go, in my seat, I did stay
The Spirit continued calling, by conviction I was fraught
My mind began to wander, soon, I had another thought

In the battle for my soul, Satan would not relent
He convinced me there would be, another day for me to repent
The Spirit offered me one last chance, to accept God's, amazing grace
I continued to reject It, as tears rolled down my face

I shut my eyes to suppress the tears, the future, I could, not see
I would have, chosen differently, had I known death was coming for me
I left the little church thinking, I had a foolproof plan
At the time I didn't know, my life's race was almost ran

The wreck it happened quickly, I had no time, to pray
Death was there waiting, ready to take me away
My life was then over, no longer could I speak
In death my voice was silent, forgiveness, I could, not seek

Jesus had offered me salvation, He wanted to make me whole
When I said, maybe next time, I had, gambled with my soul
Death had taken and wrapped me, in its cold, dark cloak
Then dropped me in to Hell, where, in torment, I awoke

Wailing souls, and gnashing teeth, are what, I now hear
A gnawing, burning pain, I feel, I'm constantly filled with fear
These flames cannot be quenched, they are always, scorching me
I will never be rescued, from this fiery, burning sea

In this sea of torment, the worm does not die
It gnaws at me constantly, for relief, I beg and cry
I beg, plead, cry, and scream, but, relief does not come
To this pain and torment, I will never, succumb

My mouth is dry, my tongue is parched
From searing pain, my body is arched
I beg for a drop, of water, I plead for a moment of leave
But from this, horrific agony, I get no reprieve

In this desolation and peril, I will forever groan
I know, there, are others here, but, I feel so alone
Trapped in this dark abyss, from the shackles, I can't break free
Separated from God, forever, He, no longer hears, my plea

I could have chosen Jesus, and lived in eternal peace

But I rejected Him, now my torment, will never cease
If, I had gone to Heaven, I could rest by the cool, gentle stream
Instead, I'm in a burning Hell, where, all I do is scream

My screams they do echo, as I beg to escape my plight
I'm surrounded by darkness, darker than the blackest night
Grace does not exist here, mercy cannot be found
In this pit of darkness, I'm now forever, bound

I am suffering misery, into eternity my torment extends
I will never get, another chance, I can no longer, make amends
The choice, I made, is forever, it can never, be undone
I rejected, Jesus, God's only, begotten Son

It is now, too late for me, this torment, I can't evade
But my friend, I'm begging you, don't make, the mistake I made
Please accept Jesus, the only One, Who can redeem
On earth, your heart may whisper, but in Hell, your soul will scream

Alphabetical Index of Poems

COLOPHON

Whispers of the Soul Christian Poetry Book Five in the Heart and Soul Christian Poetry Collection is independently published.